VONNEGUT
by the Dozen

VONNEGUT

by the Dozen

Edited by RICHARD LINGEMAN

Nation.

First printing 2013

ISBN 978-1-940489-05-6 paperback
ISBN 978-1-940489-04-9 e-book

Book design by Omar Rubio.
Printed by BookMobile in the United States and
CPi Books Ltd in the United Kingdom.

TABLE OF CONTENTS

INTRODUCTION

RICHARD LINGEMAN

At the time of Kurt Vonnegut's death in 2007, critics dismissed his body of work as another overhyped product of the 1960s counterculture, popular among shaggy youths with callow taste. But his best deals with ultimate questions, such as death and the end of the world. Perhaps the problem was that he avoided the High Seriousness demanded by some critics.

He wrote in a kind of faux simpleminded style—reminiscent, perhaps, of the German satirical novel *Simplicissimus*, whose hero is a simpleton enduring the horrors of the Thirty Years War. What he had to tell us—drawing on his own experience, his vision of life itself, however muffled in sardonic humor—was at times dark and bleak. In an essay (among the dozen he contributed to *The Nation* between 1978 and 1998) on the popular science fiction author Stanislaw Lem, Vonnegut comments, "I do not think Lem would have as many readers as he does…if he did not go to such lengths to say, in effect, what bitter night club comics often say: 'Only kidding, folks.'"

As a particularly toxic form of human stupidity, war aroused his fiercest ire. He'd fought in World War II and witnessed horrors no 17-year-old kid from Indiana could have been prepared to witness. Still, he did not avoid in his art some of the darkest topics of the benighted twentieth century, including the Allied saturation bombing of Dresden, unjustified by military necessity, which killed thousands of civilians as well as demolishing a medieval cultural landmark. As he once wrote, "I am moved to suspect now that most of our finest humorists, including Mark Twain, may have been not especially funny people who painstakingly learned their clowning only in order to seem insincere when speaking dismally of the future of mankind" ("The Necessary Miracle").

Congenitally gloomy, he suspected that among humans, thanatos—the death wish—was dominant because they really only wanted a ticket out. In "The Worst Addiction" he writes, "Compulsive preparers for World War III, in this country or any other, are as tragically and, yes, as repulsively addicted as any stockbroker passed out with his head in a toilet in the Port Authority bus terminal."

Yet he advertised himself as a "Christ-worshiping agnostic," who thought Jesus' teaching of mercy in the Sermon on the Mount was "the best idea our civilization has yet produced" (see "Hypocrites You Shall Always Have With You" and John Leonard's tribute). Sermons on the Mount do not always translate into humor and Kurt was one of a long line of German-American free thinkers. So instead of becoming a preacher, he became a satirist of the darker hue. To him humor was a metaphysical coping strategy. As he writes in another essay in this compilation, "Laughter and tears are both responses to frustration and exhaustion, to the futility of thinking and striving anymore. I myself prefer to laugh, since there is less cleaning-up to do afterward—and since I can start thinking and striving again that much sooner."

Which makes it in an odd way appropriate that Vonnegut's connection to *The Nation* rose out of an earlier acquaintanceship with the magazine's former editor and publisher Victor Navasky, through the satirical magazine *Monocle*, which Navasky helped found at Yale Law School in the 1950s. Victor recalled that he first read Vonnegut as an undergraduate at Swarthmore College, where *Player Piano* was on the optional reading list in a political science course. He mentioned this in the begging letter he sent to Vonnegut, who jokingly replied that Victor had saved his marriage by demonstrating to his first wife, Jane, a Swarthmore graduate, that he was a worthy fellow. (The marriage nevertheless ended not long after this.) His actual contribution came a few years later with a mock prospectus for a magazine about fallout shelters (this was at the time of panic in America over a possible nuclear war), which Kurt's friend and agent, Knox Burger, another acquaintance of Victor's, suggested Kurt give to *Monocle*. [1]

Flash forward to 1978, when Victor and Hamilton Fish took over *The Nation*. Victor: "Shortly after I came to *The Nation*, a friend of [assistant editor] Kai Bird's who worked in the Carter White House leaked us a year's worth of Cabinet minutes. They were boring, boring, boring, but we published a story about, and excerpts from, them and got Bob Sherrill, Marcel Ophuls and Kurt to 'review' them" (see "Message of the Leaked Minutes").

So it went, with Kurt contributing something once or

---

1 A pitch letter from Kurt to the editor of another satirical magazine called *Help!* appears in *Kurt Vonnegut Letters*, edited by Dan Wakefield. A sample: "People who are too big or too lazy or too poor to build adequate fallout shelters could buy from our company quite cheap kits guaranteed to open any shelter yet recommended by Civil Defense. The cheapest kit, selling for $14.95, say, would consist of a World War Two surplus cylinder of Cyklon B, guaranteed by I.G. Farben, and a shaped charge for blowing the lock on any shelter door. More luxurious kits might include C.D. uniforms, all-clear signals, tape recordings of beloved family pets scratching to be let in, tape recordings of old A.B.C. speeches on the harmlessness of fallout; grenades, bazookas, flamethrowers, etc."

twice a year, like a regular donation to the United Fund. *The Nation* was not his only outlet for his political writings; he was also a columnist for *In These Times*. His politics were consistently on the left, and he angrily condemned all of America's wars of choice after the one he fought in, which, for all its horrors, he considered just. During the years that Kurt wrote for *The Nation*, I, as the magazine's executive editor, worked on his contributions, though as I recall there was not much to do, except a little tidying up. I'd already met Kurt in my previous incarnation at *The New York Times Book Review*. In those days, John Leonard, editor of the *Book Review*, would hold open house around Christmas time for wassailing and carol singing. Kurt sometimes came to those affairs—a tall, slightly stooped man with sad, kindly eyes, bushy hair and a drooping moustache.

We had our home state in common—Indiana. He hailed from Indianapolis, while I was born and raised in the much smaller town of Crawfordsville, about forty-five miles west of the capital. Even after years of living in New York, I had a vestigial awe of Indianapolitans, especially those like Kurt who had attended Shortridge High School, the city's most socially and educationally prestigious public school. It was also a sports powerhouse (and regular crusher of Crawfordsville High in football) of a jock school. Dan Wakefield tells us in *Kurt Vonnegut's Letters* that he was subjected to hazing by the jock types. A cousin of mine, Raleigh Lingeman (universally known as Buzzy), was in Kurt's class, and in the course of our occasional editorial chats, he would invariably ask, "How's Buzzy?" Eventually it devolved on me to report that Buzzy had died of a heart attack.

Explaining how his high school education contributed to his later fame, Vonnegut said:

I studied public speaking at Shortridge High School in Indianapolis. That was a long time ago. At Shortridge I learned the first two rules for public speakers.... First rule: "Never read a speech." Second rule: "Never apologize." Ever since then, I have read all my speeches, and I have apologized as much as possible. I calculated that no other trained public speakers would be doing these things, and that audiences would find them refreshing novelties. In America, if you want to become famous, you must do something that everybody else has been told not to do.

From our acquaintance I got the impression that he was, like me, somewhat ambivalent about the Hoosier State, though in his later years he was well honored and remembered in his home town. The Vonneguts were a prominent family in Indianapolis: his great-grandfather founded Vonnegut Hardware, where Kurt worked summers as a boy; his grandfather and father were both well-known architects in the city. During the Great Depression, the family fortunes went south, and Kurt knew if not hardship, at least a fall from his privileged youth.

Indeed, his life was not an idyllic one even before World War II. His mother committed suicide on Mothers Day, and in later life he was hit by family tragedies. One of his sisters and her husband died within days of each other, and Kurt adopted their three children. It would not be surprising if these events colored his attitude toward life and gave his novels a mournful bass note throbbing beneath the satire and sci-fi fantasy. [2] Yet he was not a bitter man; he loved his children and regarded the world with wonder.

Somebody asked me once how come Indiana produced so many humorists (e.g., Kin Hubbard, James Whitcomb Riley, George Ade, Jean Shepherd, Herb Shriner, David Letterman, Vonnegut). I have no idea, but in Vonnegut's case Indiana gave him characters for his fiction. As he once said: "No matter where I am and how old I become, I still speak of almost nothing but my youth in Indianapolis, Indiana."

Thanks, Indiana. Writing of Mark Twain in a speech at the Mark Twain house in Hartford, Vonnegut says, "It seems clear to me, as an American writing 100 years after this house was built, that we would not be known as a nation with a supple, amusing and often beautiful language of our own, if it were not for the genius of Mark Twain." America owes Kurt Von-

---

2 He also had three children with Jane and later adopted a daughter with his second wife, the photographer Jill Krementz.

negut a similar debt for impregnating its culture with books like *Mother Night*, *Player Piano* and *Slaughterhouse 5*. And for the mordantly funny writings assembled in this collection.

Only he's not kidding, folks. ∎

Only Kidding, Folks? (1978)

A review of ten books by the Polish science-fiction writer Stanislaw Lem.

Stanislaw Lem of Cracow, born in 1921, is one of the most popular science-fiction writers in the world. Seven of his thirty or more books are available in American editions. He is among other things a physician. The American futurologist Alvin Toffler admires him, has visited him in Poland, and he tells me that Dr. Lem drives a Mercedes. So do I. Peace.

Leslie Fiedler finds him "tremendously amusing"; Gherman Titov, the Russian cosmonaut, finds him "fantastically humorous"; Ursula K. LeGuin finds him "zany," and so on. I myself find him a master of utterly terminal pessimism, appalled by all that an insane humanity may yet survive to do.

We are pollution.

He wants us to feel no pity for *Homo sapiens*, and so excludes appealing women and children from his tales. The adult males he shows us are variously bald, arthritic, sharp-kneed, squinting, jowly, rotten toothed and so on, and surely ludicrous—save for his space crewmen, who are as expendable as pawns in a chess game. We do not get to know anybody well enough to like him. If he dies, he dies.

Nowhere in the works of Jonathan Swift, even, can I find a more loathsome description of a human being than this one, taken from Lem's "Prince Ferrix and the Princess Crystal," one of a dozen fables for the Cybernetic Age in his *The Cyberiad* (Warsaw, 1967): "Its every step was like the overflowing of marshy vats, its face was like a scummy well; from its rotten breath the mirrors all covered over with a blind mist. When it spoke, it was as if a pink worm tried to squirm from its maw."

Granted: This opinion is supposedly held by a robot made of metal. But it was in fact written by a man who has presumably taken the oath of Hippocrates, a sworn treasurer of human life, and he gives me no reason in this or any other story I have read to feel regret when a human being is killed. The one in this particular fable is butchered and stuffed by the robots and put into a museum.

I do not think Lem would have as many readers as he does, including a boundlessly optimistic cosmonaut, if he did not go to such lengths to say, in effect, what bitter nightclub comics often say: "Only kidding, folks." When he predicts that our reason will soon be destroyed by mind-altering chemicals in careless hands *(The Futurological Congress,* Warsaw, 1971), or that many of our descendants will be spies or spy hunters in an underground Pentagon which has lost touch with the outside world *(Memoirs Found in a Bathtub,* Warsaw, 1971), or that, when we venture into space, we will become destroyers of all we cannot understand *(The Invincible,* Warsaw, 1967) or that our machines will soon be more intelligent and honorable than we are (the theme of tale after tale), he must be kidding, since, as LeGuin says, he is so "zany" all the time. I am moved to suspect now that most of our finest humorists, including Mark Twain, may have been not especially funny people who painstakingly learned their clowning only in order to seem insincere when speaking dismally of the future of mankind.

Yes, and as luck would have it, I have this very morning received a letter from my son Mark, a writer now completing his third year at Harvard Medical School. He says that it is a bad time for anybody's writing just now, that the spirit in the air is this: "We're destroying the planet. There's not a damn thing that can be done about it. It's going to be very slow, drawn-out and ugly, or so fast it doesn't make any difference."

So we can expect to have many more tremendously amusing writers like Stanislaw Lem. Few will be his peers in poetic exposition, in word play, and imaginative and sophisticated sympathy with machines.

A technical matter to be dealt with here: It is absolutely impossible to write a good story that does not have at least one sane and respectable character in it, someone the reader can trust. Lem gets away with such stories again and again, seemingly but not really, for he himself is never invisible. He himself is that solid character without whose presence we would not read on.

He is also no robot. So I will guess that he is at his funniest when he has looked so hard and long at hopelessness that he is at last exhausted, and is seized by convulsions of laughter that threaten to tear him to pieces. It was during such a fit that he wrote *The Futurological Congress*, I am sure—a book I have sent to Toffler, incidentally. He has not read it yet. And anyone wanting to sample Lem, hoping to like him, should probably start with that book. The hotel sheltering the congress is reduced to gravel by rioters and police, and the surviving futurologists wind up with the hotel staff in a sewer.

Laffs aplenty. Why not? ∎

MESSAGE OF THE LEAKED
MINUTES (1978)

In 1978 The Nation *obtained a copy of the minutes of President Jimmy Carter's Cabinet meetings from March 14, 1977, to March 12, 1978, and found them rather mundane. Nevertheless, they asked several writers to scrutinize them and tease out any hidden meanings or inside revelations. Here is Vonnegut's comment.*

What could a Cabinet meeting be, after all, given our society and form of government, other than an adult version of a first grade's Show and Tell? In both situations, the participants must ransack their minds for something interesting to talk about on such a day, and for the sake of talk alone. No real business can be done.

Cabinet members, like first graders, it turns out, sometimes refuse to bring anything to show or tell. At the meeting of August 1, 1977, for example, Attorney General Griffin Bell, the chief law-enforcement officer in a nation of 200 million edgy citizens, said he had nothing to report. That was it: zero. Agriculture Secretary Robert Bergland, on the other hand, was busier than a one-armed paperhanger. He said that the forest-fire season had begun, that 300 fires had already blazed up, and that more were expected. Whether anybody made the obvious suggestion, sotto voce, as to what he might do about his forest fires, we will never know.

U.N. Ambassador Andrew Young said he was going to Jamaica on Friday, and would like to talk to Bergland about sugar before he left. Defense Secretary Dr. Harold Brown said that he had been in South Korea for most of the past week, discussing details of withdrawing U.S. troops from there. And so on. There is a lack of proportion here. One child's hamster, so to speak, gets precisely as much polite attention as another child's live mortar shell from World War II.

Is this scandalous? Not at all, in my opinion—not even with Bert Lance present. And Bert Lance *was* there on the day I describe, a week or so before he was canned for questionable dealings with banks he controlled: He was extolling fiscal responsibility. He asked that ten minutes be set aside at a future meeting for a discussion of how agencies might make more realistic estimates of their future expenditures.

I, for one, am *enchanted* that the executive branch of my government should require the heads of its departments regularly to reveal themselves to one another as children—without pomp, without badges of authority—variously shy or boastful or clever or ignorant or sulky or playful or untruthful or humorless or what have you. I would not want to be a Bert Lance in such a situation. Kids can be cruel in what they secretly think about a guy when he's reciting—especially if he's fat and teacher's pet.

The Italian dictator Mussolini, I remember, had the members of *his* Cabinet jump from springboards and over hurdles of fixed bayonets in public—to demonstrate their fitness to lead. The American scheme seems simultaneously more instructive and cruel, and accidentally a Freudian masterstroke.

Subject for next week's Cabinet meeting: "What I Did Last Summer." ∎

THE NECESSARY MIRACLE (1979)

This was a speech Vonnegut delivered at Mark Twain's house in Hartford.

To every American writer this is a haunted house. My hair may turn white before this very short speech is done. I now quote a previous owner of this house: "When I find a well drawn character in fiction or biography, I generally take a warm personal interest in him, for the reason that I have known him before—met him on the river."

I submit to you that this is a profoundly Christian statement, an echo of the Beatitudes. It is constructed, as many

jokes are, incidentally, with a disarmingly pedestrian beginning and an unexpectedly provoking conclusion.

I will repeat it, for we are surely here to repeat ourselves. Lovers do almost nothing but repeat themselves.

"When I find a well-drawn character in fiction or biography, I generally take a warm personal interest in him, for the
reason that I have known him before—met him on the river."

Three words, in my opinion, make this a holy joke:
They are "warm" and "personal" and "river." The river,
of course, is life—and not just to river pilots, but even to
desert people, to people who have never even seen water
in that long and narrow form. Mark Twain is saying what
Christ said in so many ways: that he could not help loving
anyone in the midst of life.

I am of course a skeptic about the divinity of Christ and
a scorner of the notion that there is a God who cares how
we are or what we do. I was raised this way—in the midst
of what provincial Easterners imagine to be a Bible Belt. I
was confirmed in my skepticism by Mark Twain during my
formative years, and by some other good people, too. I have
since bequeathed this lack of faith and my love for the body
of literature which supports it to my children.

I am moved on this occasion to put into a few words
the ideal my parents and Twain and the rest held before Me,
and which I have now passed on. The ideal, achieved by few,

is this: "Live so that you can say to God on Judgment Day, 'I was a very good person, even though I did not believe in You." The word "God," incidentally, is, capitalized through-out this speech, as are all pronouns referring to Him.

We religious skeptics would like to swagger some in Heaven, saying to others who spent a lot of time quaking in churches down here, "I was never worried about pleasing or angering God—I never took Him into my calculations at all."

Religious skeptics often become very bitter toward the end, as did Mark Twain. I do not propose to guess now as to why he became so bitter. I know why I will become bitter. I will finally realize that I have had it right all along: that I will not see God, that there is no Heaven or Judgment Day.

I have used the word "calculations." It is a relative of that elegant Missouri verb, "to calculate." In Twain's time, and on the frontier, a person who calculated this or that was asking that his lies be respected, since they had been arrived at by means of arithmetic. He wanted you to acknowledge that the arithmetic, the logic of his lies, was sound.

I know a rowdy joke which is not fit to tell in mixed company in a Victorian home like this one. I can reveal the final line of it, however, without giving offense. This is it: "Keep your hat on. We may wind up miles from here." Any writer beginning a story might well say that to himself: "Keep your hat on. We may wind up miles from here."

This is the secret of good storytelling: to lie, but to keep the arithmetic sound. A storyteller, like any other sort of enthusiastic liar, is on an unpredictable adventure. His initial lie, his premise, will suggest many new lies of its own. The storyteller must choose among them, seeking those which are most believable, which keep the arithmetic sound. Thus does a story generate itself.

The wildest adventure with storytelling, with Missouri calculation, of which I know is *A Connecticut Yankee in King Arthur's Court*. It was written in this sacredly absurd monument—as were *The Adventures of Tom Sawyer, A Tramp Abroad, The Prince and the Pauper, Life on the Mississippi*, from which I have quoted, and the world masterpiece *Huckleberry Finn*. Twain's most productive years were spent here—from the time he was 39 until he was my age, which is 56. He was my age when he left here to live in Europe and Redding and New York, his greatest work behind him.

That is how far down the river of life he was when he left here. He could not afford to live here anymore. He was very bad at business.

About *A Connecticut Yankee:* its premise, its first lie, seemed to promise a lark. What could be more comical than sending back into the Dark Ages a late-nineteenth-century optimist and technocrat? Such a premise was surely the key to a treasure chest of screamingly funny jokes and situations. Mark Twain would have been wise to say to himself as he picked up that glittering key, "Keep your hat on. We may wind up miles from here."

I will refresh your memories as to where he wound up, with or without his hat. The Yankee and his little band of electricians and mechanics and what-have-you are being attacked by thousands of English warriors armed with swords and spears and axes. The Yankee has fortified his position with a series of electric fences and a moat. He also has several precursors to modern machine guns, which are Gatling guns.

Comically enough, thousands of early attackers have already been electrocuted. Ten thousand of the greatest knights in England have been held in reserve. Now they come. I quote, and I invite you to chuckle along with me as I read:

"The thirteen gatlings began to vomit death into the fated ten thousand. They halted, they stood their ground a moment against that withering deluge of fire, and then they broke, faced about, and swept toward the ditch like chaff before a gale. A full fourth part of their force never reached the top of the lofty embankment; the three-fourths reached it and plunged over—to death by drowning.

"Within ten short minutes after we had opened fire, armed resistance was totally annihilated, the campaign was ended, we fifty-four were masters of England! Twenty-five thousand men lay dead around us."

End quote.

What a funny ending.

Mark Twain died in 1910, at the age 75 and four years before the start of World War I. I have heard it said that he predicted that war and all the wars after that in *A Connecticut Yankee*. It was not Twain who did that. It was his premise.

How appalled this entertainer must have been to have his innocent joking about technology and superstition lead him inexorably to such a ghastly end. Suddenly and horrifyingly, what had seemed so *clear* throughout the book was not clear at all—who was good, who was bad; who was wise, who was foolish. I ask you: "Who was most crazed by superstition and, bloodlust, the men with the swords or the men with the Gatling guns?"

And I suggest to you that the fatal premise of A *Connecticut Yankee* remains a chief premise of Western civilization, and increasingly of world civilization, to wit: the sanest, most likable persons, employing superior technology, will enforce sanity throughout the world.

Shall I read the ending of *A Connecticut Yankee* to you yet again?

No need.

To return to mere storytelling, which never harmed anyone: it is the premise which shapes each story, yes, but the author must furnish the language and the mood.

It seems clear to me, as an American writing 100 years after this house was built, that we would not be known as a nation with a supple, amusing and often beautiful language of our own, if it were not for the genius of Mark Twain. Only a genius could have misrepresented our speech and our wittiness and our common sense and our common decency so handsomely to ourselves and the outside world.

He himself was the most enchanting American at the heart of each of his tales. We can forgive this easily, for he managed to imply that the reader was enough like him to be his brother. He did this most strikingly in the *personae* of the young riverboat pilot and Huckleberry Finn. He did this so well that the newest arrival to these shores, very likely a Vietnamese refugee, can, by reading him, begin to imagine that he has some of the idiosyncratically American charm of Mark Twain.

This is a miracle. There is a name for such miracles, which is "myths."

Imagine, if you will, the opinion we would now hold of ourselves and the opinions others would hold of us, if it were not for the myths about us created by Mark Twain. You can then begin to calculate our debt to this one man.

One man. Just one man.

I named my first-born son after him.

I thank you for your attention.   ■

HYPOCRITES YOU ALWAYS HAVE WITH YOU (1980)

I am enchanted by the Sermon on the Mount. Being merciful, it seems to me, is the only good idea we have received so far. Perhaps we will get another idea that good by and by—and then we will have two good ideas. What might that second good idea be? I don't know. How could I know? I will make a wild guess that it will come from music somehow. I have often wondered what music is and why we love it so. It may be that music is that second good idea's being born.

I choose as my text the first eight verses of *John 12*, which deal not with Palm Sunday but with the night before—with Palm Sunday Eve, with what we might call

"Spikenard Saturday." I hope that will be close enough to Palm Sunday to leave you more or less satisfied. I asked an Episcopalian priest the other day what I should say to you about Palm Sunday itself. She told me to say that it was a brilliant satire on pomp and circumstance and high honors in this world. So I tell you that.

The priest was Carol Anderson, who sold her physical church in order that her spiritual parish might survive.

Now, as to the verses about Palm Sunday Eve: I choose them because Jesus says something in the eighth verse which many people I have known have taken as proof that Jesus himself occasionally got sick and tired of people who needed mercy all the time. I read from the Revised Standard Bible rather than the King James, because it is easier for me to understand. Also, I will argue afterward that Jesus was only joking, and it is impossible to joke in King James English. The funniest joke in the world, if told in King James English, is doomed to sound like Charlton Heston.

I read:

Six days before the Passover, Jesus came to Bethany, where Lazarus was, whom Jesus had raised from the dead. There they made him supper; Martha served, but Lazarus was one of those at table with him.

Mary took a pound of costly ointment of pure nard and anointed the feet of Jesus and wiped his feet with her hair;

and the house was filled with the fragrance of the ointment.

But Judas Iscariot, one of his disciples (he who was to betray him), said, "Why was this ointment not sold for three hundred denarii and given to the poor?" This he said, not that he cared for the poor but because he was a thief, and, as he had the money box, he used to take what was put into it.

Jesus said, "Let her alone, let her keep it for the day of my burial. The poor you always have with you, but you do not always have me."

Thus ends the reading, and, although I have promised a joke, there is not much of a chuckle in there anywhere. The reading, in fact, ends with at least two quite depressing implications: that Jesus could be a touch self-pitying, and that he was, with his mission to Earth about to end, at least momentarily sick and tired of hearing about the poor.

The King James version of the last verse, by the way, is almost identical: "For the poor always ye have with you; but you do not always have me."

Whatever it was that Jesus really said to Judas was said in Aramaic, of course—and has come to us through Hebrew and Greek and Latin and archaic English. Maybe he only said something a lot like, "The poor you always have with you, but you do not always have me." Perhaps a little something has been lost in translation. And let us remember, too, that in translations jokes are commonly the first things to go.

I would like to recapture what has been lost. Why? Because I, as a Christ-worshiping agnostic, have seen so much un-Christian impatience with the poor encouraged by the quotation "For the poor always ye have with you."

I am speaking mainly of my youth in Indianapolis, Indiana. No matter where I am and how old I become, I still speak of almost nothing but my youth in Indianapolis, Indiana. Whenever anybody out that way began to worry a lot about the poor people when I was young, some eminently respectable Hoosier, possibly an uncle or an aunt, would say that Jesus himself had given up on doing much about the poor. He or she would paraphrase John 12, verse 8: "The poor people are hopeless. We'll always be stuck with them." The general company was then free to say that the poor were hopeless because they were so lazy or dumb, that they drank too much and had too many children and kept coal in the bathtub, and so on. Somebody was likely to quote Kin Hubbard, the Hoosier humorist, who said that he knew a man who was so poor that he owned twenty-two dogs. And so on.

If those Hoosiers were still alive, which they are not, I would tell them now that Jesus was only joking, and that he was not even thinking much about the poor. I would tell them, too, what I don't have to tell this particular congregation, that jokes can be noble. Laughs are exactly as honorable as tears. Laughter and tears are both responses to frustration and exhaustion, to the futility of thinking and striving anymore. I myself prefer to laugh, since there is less cleaning-up to do afterward—and since I can start thinking and striving again that much sooner.

All right:

It is the evening before Palm Sunday. Jesus is frustrated and exhausted. He knows that one of his closest associates will soon betray him for money—and that he is going to be mocked and tortured and killed. He is going to feel all that a mortal feels when he dies in convulsions on the cross. His visit among us is almost over—but life must still go on for just a little while.

It is again suppertime.

His male companions for supper are themselves a mockery. One is Judas, who will betray him. The other is Lazarus, who has recently been dead for four days. Lazarus was so dead that he stunk, the Bible says. Lazarus is surely dazed, and not much of a conversationalist—and not necessarily grateful, either, to be alive again. It is a very mixed blessing to be brought back from the dead.

If I had read a little further, we would have learned that there is a crowd outside, crazy to see Lazarus, not Jesus. Lazarus is the man of the hour as far as the crowd is concerned.

Trust a crowd to look at the wrong end of a miracle every time.

There are two sisters of Lazarus there—Martha and Mary. They, at least, are sympathetic and imaginatively helpful.

Mary begins to massage and perfume the feet of Jesus Christ with an ointment made from the spikenard plant. Jesus has the bones of a man and is clothed in the flesh of a man—so it must feel awfully nice, what Mary is doing to his feet. Would it be heretical of us to suppose that Jesus closes his eyes?

This is too much for that envious hypocrite Judas, who says, trying to be more Catholic than the Pope: "Hey—this is very un-Christian. Instead of wasting that stuff on your feet, we should have sold it and given the money to the poor people."

To which Jesus replies in Aramaic: "Judas, don't worry about it. There will still be plenty of poor people left long after I'm gone."

This is about what Mark Twain or Abraham Lincoln would have said under similar circumstances.

If Jesus did in fact say that, it is a divine black joke, well suited to the occasion. It says everything about hypocrisy and nothing about the poor. It is a Christian joke, which allows Jesus to remain civil to Judas, but to chide him about his hypocrisy all the same.

"Judas, don't worry about it. There will still be plenty

of poor people left long after I'm gone."

Shall I regarble it for you? "The poor you always have with you, but you do not always have me."

My own translation does no violence to the words in the Bible. I have changed their order some, not merely to make them into the joke the situation calls for but to harmonize them, too, with the Sermon on the Mount. The Sermon on the Mount suggests a mercifulness that can never waver or fade.

This has no doubt been a silly sermon. I am sure you do not mind. People don't come to church for preachments, of course, but to daydream about God.

I thank you for your sweetly faked attention.   ∎

There Must Be More to Love than Death: A Conversation With Kurt Vonnegut (1980)

This conversation with Kurt Vonnegut is one in a series of interviews Robert K. Musil conducted on the subject of American culture and the atomic bomb. Hans Bethe, David Lilienthal and George F. Kennan are among the others who have been interviewed.

Musil: It must have been difficult to work up to a book like *Slaughterhouse 5*. How long did you think about describing an experience like Dresden?

Vonnegut: Well, it seemed a categorical imperative that I write about Dresden, the firebombing of Dresden, since it was the largest massacre in the history of Europe and I am a person of European extraction and I, a writer, had been present. I *had* to say something about it. And it took me a long time and it was painful. The most difficult thing about it was that I had forgotten about it. And I learned about catastrophes from that, and from talking to other people who had been involved in avalanches and floods and great fires, that there is some device in our brain which switches off and prevents our remembering catastrophes above a certain scale. I don't know whether it is just a limit of our nervous system, or whether it's actually a gadget which protects us in some way. But I, in fact, remembered nothing about the bombing of Dresden although I had been there, and did everything short of hiring a hypnotist to recover the information. I wrote to many of the guys who went through it with me saying "Help me remember" and the answer every time was a refusal, a simple flat refusal. They did not want to think about it. There was a writer in *Life* magazine—I don't know how much he knows about rabbits and the nervous system—who claimed that rabbits have no memory, which is one of their defensive mechanisms. If they recalled every close shave they had in the course of just an hour, life would become insupportable. As soon as they'd escaped from a Doberman pinscher, why, they forgot all about it. And they could scarcely afford to remember it.

Musil: Did the details come back to you personally when you wrote to people and studied about Dresden? You said it was painful when you started thinking about it again.

Vonnegut: After all, it was a city enormous in area and I was on the ground, and there was smoke and fire, and so I could scarcely see eight feet, and the only way to see it would be on area photographs taken with the beautiful equipment that planes had. And so it was finally British military historians who produced more and more information and finally an estimate of the casualties. East Germany would not respond to my inquiries at all. They weren't interested in the problem. Probably the most curious thing, in retrospect, is that I think that I'm the only person who gives a damn that Dresden was bombed, because I have found no Germans to mourn the city, no Englishmen. I have run into flyers of one sort or another who were in on the raid. They were rather sheepish about it, and they weren't proud of it. But I have found no one who is sorry, including the people who were bombed, although they must surely mourn relatives. I went back there with a friend and there was no German to say, "Ach, how beautiful this used to be, with the tree-lined streets and the parks." They don't give a damn. And there was a special edition of *Slaughterhouse 5* that the Franklin Library brought out. For that, I had to write a special introduction for their subscribers, and I figured out that I'm the only person who profited from the bombing of Dresden. I estimated at the time I got about $4 for each person killed.

Musil: In the course of doing this series, I've interviewed people who have observed massive bombing. You weren't a bomber, but you had direct experience with bombing. I wonder if your experience in Dresden led you to any special interest (that's a bloodless way of saying it) in Hiroshima, or in subjects like nuclear weapons. Is there some connection in your mind, as in *Cat's Cradle*?

Vonnegut: Well, the interest would have been there in any event, I think. Dresden wasn't all that instructive. It was a coincidence in my life. But I think I would have been a pacifist anyway. I'm technologically educated—I'm educated as a chemist, not as a writer. I was studying chemistry at the time and was from a technocratic family. During the Depression we really believed that scientists and engineers should be put in charge and that a technological utopia was possible. My brother, who is nine years older than I am, became a distinguished scientist. He's Dr. Bernard Vonnegut, who got a Ph.D. from the Massachusetts Institute of Technology. The flashiest thing he discovered was that silver iodide will make it snow and rain. That's his patent. He is actually a leading atmospheric chemist now.

But for me it was terrible, after having believed so much in technology and having drawn so many pictures of dream automobiles and dream airplanes and dream human dwellings, to see the actual use of this technology in destroying a city and killing 135,000 people and then to see the even more sophisticated technology in the use of nuclear weapons on Japan. I was sickened by this use of the technology that I had had such great hopes for. And so I came to fear it. You know, it's like being a devout Christian and then seeing some horrible massacres conducted by Christians after a victory. It was a spiritual horror of that sort which I still carry today.

Musil: You mentioned religious and philosophical values. At the end of *Cat's Cradle*, Bokonon is talking about writing the history of human stupidity . . .

Vonnegut: There actually is a book called that, you, know. It's called the *Short Introduction to the History of Human Stupidity*, by Walter Pitkin, and it was published during the '30s. The most horrible hypocrisy or the most terrifying hypocrisy or the most tragic hypocrisy at the center of life, I think, which no one dares mention, is that human beings don't like life. Bertrand Russell skirted that, and many psychoanalysts have too, in talking about people lusting for death. But I think that at least half the people alive, and maybe nine-tenths of them, really do not like this ordeal at all. They pretend to like it some, to smile at strangers, and to get up each morning in order to survive, in order to somehow get through it. But life is, for most people, a very terrible ordeal. They would just as soon end it at any time. And I think that is more of a problem really than greed or machismo or anything like that. You know, you talk about the dark side of life: that's really it. Most people don't want to be alive. They're too embarrassed, they're disgraced, they're frightened. I think that's the fundamental thing that's going on. Those of you with your devotion to peace and all that are actually facing people perhaps as brave and determined and resourceful and thoughtful as you are on some level. And what they really want to do is to have the whole thing turned off like a light switch.

Musil: So would you consider yourself a fatalist? Throughout your books, there is the phrase, "So it goes."

But what is that theme, that leitmotif? What does it indicate about your own thinking about where we're headed, armed with our nuclear weapons?

Vonnegut: When I'm engaged in any action I have to take into consideration that many of the people on either side of me don't care what happens next. I am mistrustful of most people as custodians of life and so I'm pessimistic on that account. I think that there are not many people who want life to go on. And I'm just a bearer of bad tidings really. You know, I just got born myself and this is what I found on this particular planet. But life is very unpopular here, and maybe it will be different on the next one.

Musil: Cat's Cradle features a narrator who is ostensibly working on a book about the day the bomb went off at Hiroshima, and trying to find out what the people did, including great scientists like Dr. Felix Hoenikker, your fictional father of the bomb. What is the germ of that novel, and why did you pick that kind of focus?

Vonnegut: I was a public relations man for the General Electric Company's research laboratory, which happens to be an extremely interesting research laboratory. As General Electric found out, it was very profitable to hire scientists from M.I.T. or Princeton or wherever and say, "Hey, you don't have to teach anymore; you can do research all day long, and we won't tell you what to do. We will simply buy you the equipment." The job required my visiting the scientists often and talking to them and asking them what they were up to. Every so often a good story would come out of it. I got to know these people, and the older ones began to trouble me a lot; not the younger ones, but the older ones began to believe the truth must be served and that they need not fear whatever they turned up in the course of their research. And a man that my brother worked with there, a Nobel Prize winner named Irving Langmuir, was more or less the model for Dr. Felix Hoenikker. Langmuir was absolutely indifferent to the uses that might be made of the truths he dug out of the rock and handed out to whoever was around. But any truth he found was beautiful in its own right, and he didn't give a damn who got it next.

I think we live more according to literary stereotypes and dramatic stereotypes than we know. I think there were literary models then of pure scientists and their absent-mindedness, and jokes about the absent-minded professor and all that, and many scientists gladly fell into this stereotype of absentmindedness and indifference, including indifference as to what became of their discoveries. That generation was not cautious at all about what information it turned over to the Government, to the War Department, to the Secretary of the Army or whomever. But one member of that generation, Norbert Weiner, published an article in *The Atlantic* not long after the war was over, saying, "I'm not going to tell my Government anything anymore." And I think scientists have become more and more cautious since. I know my brother has. He was deeply chagrined to find out that the Air Force had been spewing silver iodide all over Vietnam in an effort to bring those people to their knees. You know this is preposterous. He says they might as well have been spewing paprika or something like that, hoping this would have some horrible effect on the enemy. But it sickened him to hear that they had hoped that his invention would have some destructive use.

Musil: If one of the problems as you saw it after the war was technocrats gone wild, what alternative do you propose in your literature or in your own thinking? What did you decide was the opposite or the antidote to the Felix Hoenikkers of the world?

Vonnegut: Well, I encourage restraint. I think the trouble with Dresden was restraint surely, or lack of restraint, and I don't regard technocrats as having gone mad. I think the politicians went mad, as they often do. The man responsible for the bombing of Dresden against a lot of advice was Winston Churchill. It's the brain of one man, the rage of one man, the pride of one man, and I really can't hold scientists particularly responsible for that.

Musil: But you do say, or at least the narrator says in *Cat's Cradle*, that Hoenikker couldn't have been all that innocent if he was the father of the A-bomb.

Vonnegut: Well, what I feel about him now is that he was allowed to concentrate on one part of life more than any human being should be allowed to do. He was over-specialized and became amoral on that account. It would seem perfectly all right to see a musician vanish into his own world entirely. But if a scientist does this, he can inadvertently become a very destructive person.

Musil: How do you view a subject like the threat of nuclear war? Do you think the threat is increasing and do you worry about that?

Vonnegut: Well, yes, indeed I do. I worry again about the indifference of people to it. You can talk about the various readings of *Dr. Strangelove* in that movie, and I tell you that the thing that satisfied the audience most was the beautiful end of the world, and playing that sentimental song over it. It was meant to be irony, but to most people in the audience and on most people's level it was beautiful. And I don't mean simple-minded people. I mean that this was stirring and lovely and appealing—the end of the world—and did not cause anyone to recoil from it. Now, there has been one bombing picture which does make you recoil from war, which is *The War Game*. That was extraordinary, and that was intolerable to people because it revealed how slow the death was going to be, the slow death of children and that sort of thing. That was bad news to people, but the peaceful end, the painless end was deeply gratifying to people, more so than all the Peter Sellers acting triumphs, more than the great Keenan Wynn jokes or shooting the coin box off the Coca-Cola machine. I'm afraid that beautiful ending is the reason that picture is so loved. Inadvertently, or maybe on purpose, Kubrick made a picture which sent people home utterly satisfied. And I'm sure that everyone that ever sees that picture sleeps soundly afterward and feels nothing more needs to be done.

Musil: How about your books, particularly *Slaughterhouse 5?* How do you think people react to the sort of destruction depicted there?

Vonnegut: I have really no way of knowing. I haven't talked to that many readers, but I do hear from young people who say, "My father says the war wasn't that way at all." And the German response to it has been, "No, no, the war wasn't like that." Of course, damn it, I did as good research as they did about what the war was like and what the bombing of Dresden was like. But the Germans feel, you know, it's more or less their copyrighted war, and how dare I comment on it.

Musil: Apart from your role as a writer, do you concern yourself in other ways with the matter of nuclear weapons and their proliferation?

Vonnegut: Well, for one thing, I've reproduced. I have children and I'm very fond of them and I want them to like life. I don't want them to lose heart. As for nuclear weapons, I can't imagine why anyone wants them. I don't want my country to have them. I don't want anybody to have them. And there's no point in going country by country by country because if they exist anywhere, they threaten the entire planet. So I don't want my planet to have them, and I think the people who don't feel they are particularly dangerous must be imbeciles or hypocrites. Or again, perhaps they're sick enough to want an end to life.

Musil: But what about a lively man like John F. Kennedy? Have you thought about his behavior during the Cuban missile crisis and ever wondered what was going on with someone who could sit there and say, Well, we might just have to do it?

Vonnegut: Well, this is the hypocrisy I'm talking about. When I see people with a lust for life climbing mountains or going hand over hand and doing these great acts of derring-do, showing their teeth, you know, and gnashing their teeth and loving steaks and loving women and loving whiskey and loving all of this, I become somewhat alarmed because I think perhaps that is a symptom of the hypocrisy—a person who pretends to like life and in fact overdoes it as though he or she had something to hide.

Musil: Since you have spent many years trying to understand both an event like the bombing of Dresden and the nature of scientists who could make Ice Nine or father atomic bombs, what do you think about when you hear the language of policy-makers, people who talk about the bomb or nuclear weapons as a deterrent and so on?

Vonnegut: Only about their willingness to lie, it being a normal part of politics to lie. I have a friend I went through the war with. We were scouts together, and then we were prisoners of war together. He's since become a district attorney in Pennsylvania; he's a guy named Bernie O'Hare. We came home on a troopship together and got off at Newport News. I said, "All right, what did you learn from it?" meaning World War II. We were both privates. He thought a minute and said, "I'll never believe my Government again."

During the '30s when we grew up, we did believe our Government and were great enthusiasts for it because the economy was being reborn. We were such cooperative citizens that it turned out to be a rather minor thing that made us decide that we couldn't believe our Government anymore—that we had caught it lying. It was quite something to catch your Government lying then. What it was all about was our bombing techniques. They said we had these magnificent bombsights which would allow us to drop a bomb down a smoke stack, and that there was all this microsurgery going on on the ground. Then we saw what it really was. They would send a cloud of airplanes over and bomb the shit out of everything. There was no use of bombsights whatsoever, there was simply carpet bombing. And that was kept secret from the American people: the nature of the air raids and random bombings, the shooting and the blowing up of anything that moved.

Musil: Did you accept the official Truman-Stimson explanation of the bombing of Hiroshima at first, or was that a fairly transparent lie to you?

Vonnegut: I had already gotten off the troopship. I was liberated in May and didn't get home until the middle of June. But the bomb was dropped in August, and I was home on leave then. I had seen bombings, so when Truman spoke of marshaling yards and all these other military targets that had to be hit there in Hiroshima, I knew what bullshit it was, because anything is a marshaling yard, any building that stands is an offense, any wire that still hangs between two poles is an offense. But there are all these names that can be given to them. What sticks in my mind is that Truman had talked about the targets we had been after at Hiroshima, and spoke of the marshaling yards. You know there are marshaling yards in New York and there are marshaling yards in Indianapolis and there are marshaling yards in South Bend. I think they're just railroad yards, but there's this terrible thing if you marshal in them.

Musil: To move to the present, when you heard Jimmy Carter say in his inaugural address, "We hope to move toward our ultimate goal of zero nuclear weapons," did you automatically dismiss the statement? Do you think the public has begun to expect dishonest language from Government leaders?

Vonnegut: Well, it's *thoughts* which are not taken seriously now. Orwell dealt in detail with language and the misuse of words. But he's talking about euphemisms, which is just disguising an unpleasant truth. As a matter of fact, if you go over a euphemistic sentence and put it into street English, well, then you can learn from it. You can simply decode it and get an offensive truth out of it. But I'm just talking about lies. There's no need for euphemisms anymore. The day of euphemisms is over. Now we hear total untruths. So there's no way to really crack the code except to suspect that the intent was to deceive.

Musil: Let me turn to a final question. Is there a way to let people know about the nuclear threat, really know that the world may blow up, without turning them off psychologically? Suppose I came to you for advice and said, "Look, I would like to alert people that there are these nuclear weapons out there and I might do a movie or write some poetry or go give speeches—how can it best be done?"

Vonnegut: You are, and people like you are, crying in the wilderness and everything else is a rock or a tree, I think. And again, as I say, there are very few enthusiasts for life. It's as though you were just crazy about mah-jongg. If everybody would play mah-jongg, again, this might bring back the mah-jongg rage of the '20s. And, Jesus, nobody else will look at the tiles or pay any attention; they don't care. They're not into that particular sport, and your particular sport is survival. It's one more game, and most people don't care to play.

Musil: What does that lead *you* to conclude? Since your experience in World War II, we've gone from block-busters then single so-called puny atomic bombs of only twelve kilotons, to megatons, and now there are some 50,000 of them in the world. Do you ever think personally, "We're not going to make it"?

Vonnegut: Well, we have made it. I mean, here we are. We're still alive, aren't we? We have survived, and how long we're supposed to do this, I don't know. It seems to me the whole world is living like Alcoholics Anonymous now, which is one day at a time, and it seems to me that President Carter is living that way too. Every night when he goes to bed he cackles, "By God, we made it through another day! Everybody said I was a lousy President, and here we've survived another day. That's not bad." We are living day by day by day now, but there seems to be very little restraint in the world. What an alcoholic does every day is not take a drink, and only not take a drink for a day. But I see no real restraint with regard to warlike actions. If we were truly interested in surviving, and having sobriety, each day we would congratulate ourselves not for merely having gotten through another day but for making it without a warlike gesture. But there is no such restraint. More weapons are manufactured every day and more arguments are gladly entered into and more enormous, dangerous lies are told, so there is no restraint. It would be truly wonderful if we could live as alcoholics do, to be unwarlike for just another day. We don't. We're totally warlike, and sooner or later something's going to go wrong. The book I'm working on now is about a kid, he's grown now, grown and in his 40s and his father was a gun nut. It was a house with dozens of guns in it. At the age of 11 this kid was playing with one of his father's guns, which he wasn't supposed to do, put a cartridge into a 30-06 rifle and fired out a goddamn attic window and killed a housewife, you know, eighteen blocks away, just drilled her right between the eyes. And this has colored his whole life, and made his reputation. And of course this weapon should not have existed. He was brought into a planet where this terribly unstable device existed, and all he had to do was sneeze near it. I mean, it wanted to be fired; it was built to be fired. It had no other purpose than to be fired and the existence of such an unstable device within the reach of any sort of human being is intolerable. ∎

A RELUCTANT
BIG SHOT (1981)

A friend recently played a tape for me which he had made at the press conference when Bill Leonard, head of CBS News, announced that Dan Rather would succeed Walter Cronkite as anchorman and managing editor of CBS Evening News, a job Cronkite had held for nineteen years. The mood of the occasion was almost randomly solemn or businesslike or playful—as though no one could be certain as to how seriously the changeover should be taken. The principal concern, I sensed, was for the American people. There seemed a chance that Cronkite had accidentally become our electronic monarch, in which case this ordinary corporate event, the semi-retirement of an employee at the age of 65, had better sound a little like an abdication followed by a coronation—which it did.

Rather was the most solemn of all, and that is nothing against him. I don't see how he could have gotten out of being humble yet brave, and so on.

But that was a year ago. The actual crisis is upon us. On March 6, Cronkite vanishes from the Evening News, as promised. This is a test of how crazy television can make us, or fail to make us, and the news is good. I can find no one who feels that we are losing a leadership figure of any sort. The people have somehow managed to keep Cronkite nicely in scale—with a lot of help from Cronkite himself. A subliminal message in every one of his broadcasts was that he had no power and wanted none. So now we feel that a kindly and intelligent teacher is leaving our village. It turns out not to matter that the village happens to be as big as all outdoors.

I have seen Cronkite laugh like Father Christmas when he is told that he should run for President or Vice President or Senator. No one ever seems to mention a governorship or a seat in the House of Representatives. I have also noticed that nobody else laughs much at the joke, even when Cronkite explains it—when he says that he is only a newsman, without any of the gifts and enthusiasms good leaders have. He intimated in a recent interview that he hadn't even aspired to be a big shot in television, that he would have been nearly as contented as he is today if he had remained what he was in the beginning—a print journalist of no great fame. He loves his family. He loves his friends. He loves his sailboat. And he remains as entranced by the unfolding of each day's news as a child with a new kaleidoscope.

What makes it hard for others to laugh along with him is that this is the land of opportunity, and no one here is supposed to fail to snatch any opportunity that is unlucky enough to be caught in the open. Walter Cronkite could have been President of this country, just as George Washington in his own day could have become King. All he had to do was to lose his temper in public, and to pick a side:

"This is Walter Cronkite, born in Joplin, Missouri, and raised in Texas, and you all know me, and I am fed to the teeth with all the stupidity and greed I see in Washington. I can no longer sit by idly. . ." And so on.

His last name is Dutch, by the way—like Roosevelt.

Morley Safer, Cronkite's CBS colleague for the past fifteen years, said the other day that he expected local rather than national television news people to transmute their popularity into hard-edged political power. I thought at once of a young man of my acquaintance who had been a star reporter a few years back on a local show here in New York City. At the age of 30, he concluded in all seriousness that he should run for mayor, and that nobody could stop him.

"Why should you be mayor?" I asked him.

"Because nobody can jive me," he replied.

The young man was a famous crusader. Cronkite is not. He may still become one, although I myself do not particularly recommend it, but he has so far done nothing to match, for example, Edward R. Murrow's vivisection of Senator Joseph McCarthy on the air. Cronkite's lack of rudeness to any political faction over so many years may have had a curious side effect, as unwelcome to him, I'm sure, as it should be to all of us: he may have encouraged us to imagine that there is a sort of sanity and wisdom on which all Americans can and should agree. Cronkite is not our electronic monarch—but he just might, accidentally, have become our electronic Uncle Sam.

No, Virginia, this is an acrimoniously pluralistic society. There is no Uncle Sam.

I asked Safer if there were any particular political issues in which Cronkite had felt personally involved year after year. He said that Cronkite, as a public speaker off the air, is regularly angry and disgusted and alarmed over anyone, no matter how powerful or popular, who would in any way limit the freedom of the press.

This, I submit, is not how Uncle Sam talks. It is the romantic stubbornness of an old newspaperman.

Safer said, too, that when he worked under him, Cronkite declared with utmost sincerity that his assistants were doing all the work, and that the investigating they were doing out in the world was what he himself most loved to do.

This is the raffish gallantry of an old newspaperman.

Cronkite steps aside just as old newspapermen are becoming as legendary as cowboys. As young as this country is, we will have a rich mythology by and by. Radio and television news began with old newspaper people. How else could they have begun?

The noun "press" is now archaic as applied to news editors and reporters. Equally antique is the cliché that describes Walter Cronkite so well:

"He has printer's ink in his veins." ∎

Stars and Bit Players (1981)

Vonnegut made this speech at the Eugene V. Debs home in Terre Haute, Indiana, upon receiving an annual award, presented by the Debs foundation.

I studied public speaking at Shortridge High School in Indianapolis. That was a long time ago.

It was well before the founding of the John Birch Society in Indianapolis. It was about the time of William Dudley Pelley and his Silver Shirts.

A lot of people don't take my hometown as seriously as they should. But then I tell them it is the world's largest city not on a navigable waterway, and the first place in America where a white man was hanged for the murder of an Indian. It is probably also the last place where a white man was hanged for the murder of an Indian. Indianapolis is more than just a Speedway with the Eli Lilly Company in the infield. It takes one heck of a lot more than a Speedway, and the Eli Lilly Company to produce a James Whitcomb Riley or the Rev. Jim Jones.

At Shortridge I learned the first two rules for public speakers. Jim Jones probably knew them, too. First rule: "Never read a speech." Second rule: "Never apologize."

Ever since then, I have read all my speeches and I have apologized as much as possible. I calculated that no other trained public speakers would be doing these things, and that audiences would find them refreshing novelties. In America, if you want to become famous, you must do something that everybody else has been told not to do.

In fact, we are in the home now of a man who was told along with everybody else, "Whatever you do, don't gum up the railroads. They are the lifelines of our mighty nation." So he became famous by gumming up the lifelines of our mighty nation.

After that, he tried to gum up the First World War. If he were alive today, he would probably try to gum up the Third World War. Anything for fame.

Now it is time for an apology—two apologies, actually.

My first apology is for accepting an award named after a labor hero. I am no labor hero. The Eugene V. Debs Award should always go to a working stiff, but it's too late now. One thing I can give you my word of honor about, anyway: I have never crossed a picket line and I will never cross a picket line. I would rather be dead.

Am I from a liberal family? Not strikingly so. As I reported in the introduction to my novel *Jailbird*, my father, an Indianapolis architect, was startled to learn in 1945 that there had been some doubt about the guilt of Sacco and Vanzetti.

My first ancestor in this country, my great-great-grandfather Jacob Schramm, who cleared a farm in Sugar Creek Township, Hancock County, wrote to a friend in Bavaria in 1842: "It appears that human weakness makes it impossible to sustain a republic on this earth for any length of time, and the majority of people need, necessarily, a driving leader without whom they will inevitably wind up in chaos. Nevertheless, the Americans are still very proud of their freedom, even though they are the worst slaves, and there is sure to be a bloody revolution before a monarchic government can gain a foothold here."

What radicalized me? What made me think that the Bill of Rights was more than a scrap of paper? A splendid education in the Indianapolis public schools, plus the Great

Depression, plus three years as a private in the Army.

What radicalizes Americans? America.

Apology number two: I am sorry for the damage that storytellers have done to the minds of the young. This is not my surrender to the Moral Majority, which burns my books. I will continue in my writing to hint where babies really come from, and that God shouldn't be put in charge of everything until we get to know Him a little better, and that our exalted leaders are just like a lot of nitwits I went to high school with, and that American soldiers have been known to curse when wounded, and so on. I don't apologize for any of that.

I apologize for all the stories and plays that have taught young people that there are stars and bit-part players, and that the stars are all that matter. Look! There is the Emperor Napoleon crossing a battlefield after a victory—astride his dapple-gray. What are all those heaps of rags on the ground? Those are bit-part players, dying or dead. And who is this being borne toward the Emperor in a sedan chair, covering her ears so that she can't hear the groans of the bit-part players? It is the Empress Josephine! What lips! What eyes!

While I am at it, let me apologize for chess sets, too, with all those pawns so obviously born to be sacrificed. It is nothing to lose a pawn. It can even be fun—in a gambit. But losing a king: that's something else again.

But writers can't be held responsible for the seeming moral lessons inherent in chess sets. So I withdraw my apology for chess.

I confess, however, to having written plenty of stories in which some characters are made to seem a lot more vital to civilization than others—stories with kings and pawns, so to speak. Almost all writers tell stories like that. But we don't tell such stories because we think life is like that or should be like that. We do it in order to hold the attention of our audience. It is a purely technical matter. An audience cannot care equally about dozens of characters all at once. It gets confused and then bored, having lost track of who is who. So we give all the important actions and speeches to just a few characters. We create stars. We say in effect to our audiences, "Just keep your eyes on the stars, and get to know a little something about them, and you won't miss anything."

One of the few writers who got away from this pernicious scheme just a little bit was that great socialist George Bernard Shaw. Another was that great humanitarian, the physician Anton Chekhov. But neither one of them got all that far away from it.

And I call it a pernicious scheme because it is shockingly clear to me now that people have so mingled stories and real life in their minds that they imagine that in real life there are stars on the one hand and, on the other hand, people who do not matter. This will not do anywhere on earth, but it particularly will not do in America, which is struggling toward democracy. How tragic it is in our would-be democracy for it to be widely believed that most of us can be as casually sacrificed as pawns.

Send the pawns to fight in Vietnam. Send them here, send them there—send them anywhere. Or forget they exist. That's O.K., too.

We are not supporting characters in the cast of *Hamlet*, ready for any sort of humiliation or death, if only the Prince of Denmark can learn a thing or two.

I first thought of making this apology ten years ago, at the time of the riots and then the massacre of convicts and hostages alike at the Attica Correctional Facility in upstate New York. What happened at Attica was at least a statistical curiosity. It was the largest massacre of Americans by Americans since the Civil War. Forty-three Americans were killed by Americans.

What caught my eye, though, was the behavior of Nelson Rockefeller, then Governor of New York. The situation was this: He was in Albany while at Attica, convicts had taken over much of the prison, including one of four courtyards. They had also captured fifty prison employees, whom they were holding as hostages. This was an extremely dangerous situation. Dangerous to whom? To the convicts and their hostages. The convicts and their hostages and their terrified families and friends all begged Rockefeller to come to Attica—to exert the magic and grace inherent in his office as governor so as to make it possible, somehow, for no one to die. He was asked to risk his dignity, and perhaps even his body, in order that some lives be saved. This is a familiar enough sort of summons to other sorts of public servants—to policemen and firemen and soldiers.

But Nelson Rockefeller proudly declined to come. Instead, he sent state troopers in with their weapons blazing, firing at anything that looked like a human being. Ten of the forty-five killed were hostages. Some rescue!

Ten years ago.

Why didn't Nelson Rockefeller go to Attica? Because he believed himself to be a leading character in a story, I think—the only leading character in this case. Nobody else famous was involved. Nobody else had a name that was familiar from coast to coast.

Nelson Rockefeller honestly believed that if anything demeaning happened to him, the star of the Attica story, the story would become confusing and boring to the audience. It would stop being a wonderful story. So he refused to go to Attica, and he ordered the state troopers to open fire indiscriminately on all the bit-part players instead.

Did it bother him much that so many of the nobodies who were killed and wounded were virtuous hostages rather than wicked convicts? There is little evidence to that effect. A dead bit-part player is a dead bit-part player, no matter what side he may have been on. Ask the Emperor Napoleon after a great victory. Ask the Empress Josephine.

Ten years ago.

Have we learned anything since then? Well, I am telling you here in Terre Haute, which means "high ground," what we should have learned, and what we had better teach our children: The star system in real life is making us as sick as dogs in spirit, and it will kill us all, if we don't watch out.

Consider the attitudes of the virtuous United States of America and the wicked Union of Soviet Socialist Republics as they deploy their rockets and warheads for World War III. The angels on our side and the devils on theirs are saying to one another, as though they were discussing some cheap and earthy resource like bauxite or coal or iron: "If we get mad enough or scared enough, we will blow all your bit-part players away."

And what is it we are hearing more and more about this seemingly inevitable and perhaps even desirable Third World War? "Don't worry. Some stars will survive. All we need is a few stars for the story to go on and on and on."

Speaking for our side, I want to say that, at a minimum, in my opinion, Bob Hope will survive. Palm Springs will survive.

So why wouldn't I apologize for literature's having been taken so seriously? I won't even get into the damage we writers have done with the endings of our tales. Events in life don't end. Only stories end. But now we storytellers have people expecting not only that events will end ever so neatly but that we will understand all sorts of things we couldn't understand before—at the end. So by all means, let us hasten to the end.

Bon voyage!

But let's forget endings tonight—for want of time. Let's stick to the star syndrome, which I consider the moral herpes of our era.

My Lord—we now have this young monster named David Stockman, who has been so impressed by fiction as to believe that bit-part players in real life needn't even have food or shelter or clothing—outside of prison or the armed forces, of course. He can't see that they even deserve work or hope.

And what can be the meaning of the lunatic displays of deluxe clothes and food and crockery in Washington, D.C., these days, but that our officials imagine themselves to be leading characters in our story? They are reassuring us that America is O.K., no matter how gruesome life is in High Ground, Indiana, since our stars are becoming happier all the time.

No end of good news from Washington, D.C.

Let Terre Haute send these ringing words to the District of Columbia: "We are not simpering gaga fans!"

How deeply infected are we all by what I have called the moral herpes of our era? Consider how inappropriate to this era, how exotic, how almost incomprehensible these words are, the most famous words ever spoken by Eugene V. Debs (has any speaker in this house ever failed to quote them?):

"While there is a lower class, I am in it; while there is a criminal element, I am of it; while there is a soul in prison, I am not free."

How many of us can echo those words and mean them? If this were a decent nation, we would all find those sentiments as natural and easy to say as "Good morning. It looks like another nice day."

But the star system has made us all ravenous for the slightest proof that we matter to the American story, somehow, at least a little bit more than someone else.

I will now parody the words of Eugene V. Debs, not to make fun of them but to bring them up to date:

"While there is a lower class, I can scorn it; while there is a criminal element, I can make war on it; while there is a soul in prison, I can imagine that I am free."

What should we do about this? We should teach our young that life is nothing like a movie or a play or a book or a television show—or a picture in a frame. Children at an early age have no trouble telling salt from pepper or apples from oranges. Let us teach them to make equally quick and sharp distinctions between life and art.

Let us tell them why some characters are more important than others in art, and that this has nothing to do with life itself. Life has no unimportant characters.

Let our children be quick to spot people who imagine that they are characters in a story, and quick to understand that not only are such people a little batty but they have often appeared in history as very bad news.

Hitler.

Caligula.

Is nobody ever to be sacrificed, pawn like, for somebody else? Of course, sacrifices will continue to be made. I only want Americans to decide for themselves to what extent, if any, they were born to be sacrificed. Many Americans, facing real dangers, will surely find themselves saying what Nelson Rockefeller should have said when he was asked by nobodies to come to Attica: "Very well—the time has come to put my life on the line. It is my duty."

I thank you for the Eugene V. Debs Award.

Tonight you have made me a star. ∎

LETTERS TO
THE YOUNG (1982)

E
rnest Callenbach has an M.A. in English from the University of Chicago, and is editor of *Film Quarterly* and an editor for the University of California Press—but he could not find a publisher for his first novel, *Ecotopia*. So he published it himself. That was back in 1975, when he was 45 years old. I mention his age because so many of his enthusiasms are popularly associated with a younger generation.

Ecotopia is about an American male journalist's travels in a new nation whose citizens waste nothing, poison nothing, work only twenty hours a week, wear patched blue jeans, smoke marijuana and run their machinery with energy from the sun, the wind, the sea and the products of fermentation. They are organic farmers. They hate auto-mobiles and nuclear power plants. They love bicycles and mass transportation.

Ecotopia could easily have been funny. It is serious in-stead. We are meant to admire the Ecotopians, and to be in-spired to live as they do.

Callenbach, to whom I have spoken on the tele-phone, is aware that the book is a lot more successful as a conservationist tract than as a novel. The plot is feeble. The journalist is prepared to find all sorts of things wrong with the new nation. But there is nothing wrong with it, and he falls in love with an Ecotopian woman, and he be-comes a citizen.

Still, Callenbach managed to sell 40,000 copies of *Ecotopia*, without advertising and without its being re-viewed in any major literary journal—and then Bantam brought out a new edition and sold 145,000 more. So he has had a nice little success, which he surely deserves. *Ec-otopia* is an admirable inducer of daydreams about what life might be like if we stopped wrecking the planet and started adoring it.

But Callenbach was no more satisfied with the book as fiction than his readers were, so he wrote *Ecotopia Emerging*, which is about the birth pangs of the new nation. Again, he had to publish it himself. He brought it out in 1981, when he was 51, and has sold 3,000 copies so far. We meet the same windmills and solar cells and wood-burning stoves and high-speed railways and so on that we got to know in *Ecotopia*. But the citizens are in an uproar this time. They are trying to secede from the United States of America. They want to take Washington and Oregon with them, and the northern half of California, including San Francisco. So they have a fight on their hands.

But they win.

They claim to have hidden atomic bombs around what is left of the United States, which they call "the old country." They promise to set the bombs off if they are attacked. Also: "the old country" is militarily engaged elsewhere, defending oil fields overseas.

During our telephone conversation, Callenbach proved to be engagingly critical of his own writings. He felt, as I do, that he was probably mistaken to have allowed his idealists to grab off such desirable real estate, leaving the rest of us stuck with their share of the national debt, and practically all the old people and poor people, and the Love Canal, and so on.

"They shouldn't have taken San Francisco," I said. "That was just too greedy. As far as I am concerned, that was the straw that broke the camel's back."

He thought I was right, but he asked me to imagine

the book he would have had to write if he had situated his Sierra Club utopia on the shores of Lake Erie, say. Such a book would have been the size of James Clavell's *Noble House*, since the cleanup of the city of Niagara Falls alone would have covered a period of a thousand years or more.

Also—although Callenbach did not say so, there would have been a lot of old people in that story, and both of his novels, more than anything else, are love letters from a middle-aged man to the innocently conceited, undisillusioned young. Everybody of any importance in his utopia is under 30 years old.

Imagine a place like that.

Here are the rules for good living that the childish leaders of his brave new world lay down, and they turn out to be the same rules agreed upon by my own children—before they themselves began to enter middle age: "No extinction of other species. No nuclear weapons or nuclear plants. No manufacturing of carcinogenic or mutagenic substances. No adulterants in foods. No discrimination by reason of sex, race, age, religion, or ethnic origin. No private cars. No limited liability corporations. No growth in population."

These good rules are called "The Nine No-nos."

And the prevailing winds bring nothing but fresh air from

the Pacific to Ecotopia, and they carry the wood smoke and marijuana fumes away.   ■

THE WORST ADDICTION OF THEM ALL (1984)

What has been America's most nurturing contribution to the culture of this planet so far? Many would say jazz. I, who love jazz, will say this instead: Alcoholics Anonymous.

I am not an alcoholic. If I was, I would go before the nearest A.A. meeting and say, "My name is Kurt Vonnegut. I am an alcoholic." God willing, that might be my first step down the long, hard road back to sobriety.

The A.A. scheme, which requires a confession like that, is the first to have any measurable success in dealing with the tendency of some human beings, perhaps 10 percent of any population sample anyone might care to choose, to become addicted to substances that give them brief spasms of pleasure but in the long term transmute their lives and the lives of those around them into ultimate ghastliness.

The A.A. scheme, which, again, can work only if the addicts regularly admit that this or that chemical is poisonous to them, is now proving its effectiveness with compulsive gamblers, who are not dependent on chemicals from a distillery or a pharmaceutical laboratory. This is no paradox. Gamblers, in effect, manufacture their own dangerous substances. God help them, they produce chemicals that elate them whenever they place a bet on simply anything.

If I was a compulsive gambler, which I am not, I would be well advised to stand up before the nearest meeting of Gamblers Anonymous and declare, "My name is Kurt Vonnegut. I am a compulsive gambler."

Whether I was standing before a meeting of Gamblers Anonymous or Alcoholics Anonymous, I would be encouraged to testify as to how the chemicals I had generated within myself or swallowed had alienated my friends and relatives, cost me jobs and houses and deprived me of my last shred of self-respect.

Not every member of A.A. or G.A. has sunk quite that low, of course—but plenty have. Many, if not most, have done what they call "hitting bottom" before admitting what it is that has been ruining their lives.

I now wish to call attention to another form of addiction, which has not been previously identified. It is more like gambling than drinking, since the people afflicted are ravenous for situations that will cause their bodies to release exciting chemicals into their bloodstreams. I am persuaded that there are among us people who are tragically hooked on preparations for war.

Tell people with that disease that war is coming and we have to get ready for it, and for a few minutes there, they will be as happy as a drunk with his martini breakfast or a compulsive gambler with his paycheck bet on the Super Bowl.

Let us recognize how sick such people are. From now on, when a national leader, or even just a neighbor, starts talking about some new weapons system which is going to cost us a mere $29 billion, we should speak up. We should say something on the order of, "Honest to God, I couldn't be sorrier for you if I'd seen you wash down a fistful of black beauties with a pint of Southern Comfort."

I mean it. I am not joking. Compulsive preparers for World War III, in this country or any other, are as tragically and, yes, as repulsively addicted as any stockbroker passed out with his head in a toilet in the Port Authority bus terminal.

For an alcoholic to experience a little joy, he needs maybe three ounces of grain alcohol. Alcoholics, when they are close to hitting bottom, customarily can't hold much alcohol.

If we know a compulsive gambler who is dead broke, we can probably make him happy with a dollar to bet on who can spit farther than someone else.

For us to give a compulsive war-preparer a fleeting moment of happiness, we may have to buy him three Trident submarines and a hundred intercontinental ballistic missiles mounted on choo-choo trains.

If Western Civilization were a person—

If Western Civilization, which blankets the world now, as far as I can tell, were a person—

If Western Civilization, which surely now includes the Soviet Union and China and India and Pakistan and on and on, were a person—

If Western Civilization were a person, we would be directing it to the nearest meeting of War-Preparers Anonymous. We would be telling it to stand up before the meeting and say, "My name is Western Civilization. I am a compulsive war-preparer. I have lost everything I ever cared about. I should have come here long ago. I first hit bottom in World War I."

Western Civilization cannot be represented by a single person, of course, but a single explanation for the catastrophic course it has followed during this bloody century is possible. We the people, because of our ignorance of the disease, have again and again entrusted power to people we did not know were sickies.

And let us not mock them now, any more than we would mock someone with syphilis or smallpox or leprosy or yaws or typhoid fever or any of the other diseases to which the flesh is heir. All we have to do is separate them from the levers of power, I think.

And then what?

Western Civilization's long, hard trip back to sobriety might begin.

A word about appeasement, something World War II, supposedly, taught us not to practice: I say to you that the world has been ruined by appeasement. Appeasement of whom? Of the Communists? Of the neo-Nazis? No! Appeasement of the compulsive war-preparers. I can scarcely name a nation that has not lost most of its freedom and wealth in attempts to appease its own addicts to preparations for war.

And there is no appeasing an addict for very long.

"I swear, man, just lay enough bread on me for twenty multiple re-entry vehicles and a fleet of B-1 bombers, and I'll never bother you again."

Most addictions start innocently enough in childhood, under agreeable, reputable auspices—a sip of champagne at a wedding, a game of poker for matchsticks on a rainy afternoon. Compulsive war-preparers may have been encouraged as infants to clap their hands with glee at a campfire or a Fourth of July parade.

Not every child gets hooked. Not every child so tempted grows up to be a drunk or a gambler or a babbler about knocking down the incoming missiles of the Evil Empire with laser beams. When I identify the war-preparers as addicts, I am not calling for the exclusion of children from all martial celebrations. I doubt that more than one child in a hundred, having seen fireworks, for example, will become an adult who wants us to stop squandering our substance on education and health and social justice and the arts and food and shelter and clothing for the needy, and so on— who wants us to blow it all on ammunition instead.

And please understand that the addiction I have identified is to *preparations* for war. I repeat: to *preparations* for war, addiction to the thrills of de-mothballing battleships and inventing weapons systems against which there cannot possibly be a defense, supposedly, and urging the citizenry to hate this part of humanity or that one, and knocking over little governments that might aid and abet an enemy someday, and so on. I am not talking about an addiction to war itself, which is a very different matter. A compulsive preparer for war wants to go to big-time war no more than an alcoholic stockbroker wants to pass out with his head in a toilet in the Port Authority bus terminal.

Should addicts of any sort hold high office in this or any other country? Absolutely not, for their first priority will always be to satisfy their addiction, no matter how terrible the consequences may be—even to themselves.

Suppose we had an alcoholic President who still had not hit bottom and whose chief companions were drunks like himself. And suppose it were a fact, made absolutely clear to him, that if he took just one more drink, the whole planet would blow up.

So he has all the liquor thrown out of the White House, including his Aqua-Velva shaving lotion. So late at night he is terribly restless, crazy for a drink but proud of not drinking. So he opens the White House refrigerator, looking for a Tab or a Diet Pepsi, he tells himself. And there, half-hidden by a family-size jar of French's mustard, is an unopened can of Coors beer.

What do you think he'll do? ∎

GOD BLESS YOU,
EDWIN MEESE (1986)

I have read much of the heart-rending testimony extracted from victims of sexual abuse at meetings of the Attorney General's Commission on Pornography. It is clear to me that our government must be given the power to suppress words and images that cause sexually motivated insanity and crimes. As the Bible says, "In the beginning was the Word." I myself make my living with words, and I am now ashamed. In view of the terrible damage freely circulated ideas can do to a society, and particularly to children, I beg my government to delete from my works all thoughts that might be dangerous. I want the help of our elected leaders in bringing my thoughts into harmony with their own and thus into harmony with the thoughts of those who elected them. That is democracy.

Attempting to make amends at this late date, I call to the attention of the Attorney General's Commission on Pornography, and God bless the Attorney General, the fundamental piece of obscenity from which all others spring, the taproot of the deadly poisonous tree. Kill the taproot and the tree dies, and with it its deadly fruits, which are rape, sodomy, wife-beating, child abuse, divorce, abortion, adultery, prostitution, syphilis, gonorrhea, herpes and AIDS.

I will read this most vile of all pieces of so-called literature aloud, so that those who dare can feel the full force of it. I recommend that all persons under 14, and all persons under 30 not accompanied by an adult, leave the room. Those remaining who have heart trouble or respiratory difficulties or who are prone to commit rape at the slightest provocation may want to stick their fingers in their ears. And what I ask you to endure so briefly now is what the selfless members of the pornography commission do day after day for the good of our children. I am simply going to dip you in filth, then pull you out and wash you off immediately. At terrible risk of infection, they have to wallow in pornography. They are so fearless. We might think of them as sort of sewer astronauts. All right. Everybody ready? Here we go:

> Congress shall make no law respecting an establishment of religion, or prohibiting the free exercise thereof; or abridging the freedom of speech, or of the press; or the right of the people peaceably to assemble, and to petition the Government for a redress of grievances.

That disgusting, godless loop of kiddie porn, friends and neighbors, happens to be a basic law of this country. How could this have happened? Some pederastic Congressman, while we weren't watching, must have tacked it onto the Rivers and Harbors bill. It should be expunged with all possible haste, in order that children may be safe again.

Adolf Hitler blamed the Jews for inspiring every sort of sexual ugliness in Germany, so he tried to kill them all. Say what you like about him, incidentally, it can't be denied that he led an exceedingly clean life sexually. In the end, he made an honest woman of his only sexual partner, Eva Braun. And it was simply an invention of British propaganda that he had only one ball.

Hitler was wrong about the Jews. It is unclean images that are responsible for unclean sexuality. In order to protect German children, all he had to do was get rid of unclean images, which is what more and more good Americans now propose we do. Before we can do that, though, we must get rid of the First Amendment. In no way can this be interpreted as an anti-Semitic act. The authors of that Amendment, Thomas Jefferson and James Madison, were not Jews.

It is not enough that sex crimes of every sort are already against the law and are punished with admirable severity. It is up to our leaders, and particularly our Attorney General, to persuade a large part of our citizenry that even the most awful sex crimes are made legal, and even celebrated in some godless quarters, because of the permissiveness of our Constitution. Only then will an aroused citizenry rise up in righteous wrath to smash the First Amendment—and many other only slightly less offensive parts of the Bill of Rights.

Once the findings of the Attorney General's Commission on Pornography are published for all to see, whether they can read or not, what sort of American would dare to defend liberty, whose cost is so horrible? I'll tell you what kind of an American, friends and neighbors: the sort of American who would rape a 3-year-old girl, drench her in lighter fluid, set her ablaze, and throw her off a fire escape.

As we used to say in geometry class back in public school

when I was a boy: "Q.E.D. —*quod erat demonstrandum.*"

I thank you for your attention.   ∎

WHAT I'D SAY IF THEY ASKED ME (1988)

Ever concerned with raising the level of political discourse in this country, we asked novelist Kurt Vonnegut to compose an acceptance speech for Michael Dukakis. Of course, writers have contributed to presidential oratory in the past, but their efforts were lost in the revision-by-committee process. Here's the real thing, unfiltered and undiluted.

I am here to serve the people of the United States of America—all of them, in all ways which are lawful. I will not now speak of my humbleness. It has been said with some truth, I suppose, that almost anyone can grow up to be President. I have to add, "But surely not an humble child." The Presidency is simultaneously a pinnacle of power and of vanity, and God help us all.

An aspect of my vanity, which seems to have found favor with a majority of those who chose to vote, is my belief that, with the help of the fourth branch of government mentioned in our Constitution, "We the people," I can do a lot to help the United States of America become the United States of America— at last, at last.

The echo of Martin Luther King in my words is intentional when I say, "At last, at last."

It will do us no harm today, as it has surely done no harm to other nations I need not name, to acknowledge a past soiled with atrocities, including, in our case, slavery and genocide, and the treatment of women of whatever race under law as though they were not citizens but property. Let us celebrate how far we have come from such bad old days in so short a time, and measure how far we have yet to go. What better measurement might we use for progress made and progress yet to come than the health and happiness and wisdom and safety of all our people? And make no mistake about it: This nation is the most astonishing and admirable experiment in pluralistic democracy in history. Because of our wealth, the fairness of our Bill of Rights and the openness of our long borders, every conceivable sort of human being is now an American.

We are the world.

There is much in the recent past I would undo, if I could, especially our overwhelming national debt, whose undoing will be slow and painful. I will try to find out what good things, if any, we bought with all that money, borrowed mostly from foreigners. I will report back to you, whose children and grandchildren must pay it back with interest. I will be surprised, as I am sure most of you will be, too, if I find many purchases our descendants might thank us for.

With your encouragement, and with the cooperation of your elected representatives, I will attempt, after listening to the best-informed advisers I can find, to give future generations reasons to think well of us after all. There you have it, the principal mission of my administration: to create and bequeath to the future a decent habitat for all, free of poisons, free of hunger, free of ignorance, free of hate.

Too much, too much?

Ah, but a man's reach should exceed his grasp,

Or what's a heaven for?

Those are the words of Robert Browning, of course. I can put it a lot less elegantly, if you like:

Company's coming! Let's clean up this mess.

Many of the poisons in the water and the air and the

topsoil are new. One which can sicken our spirit is ancient, and only since World War II has this country begun to fight it with any seriousness: the idea that females and persons of color are second-class citizens. That poison would love to make a great big comeback, to take its lethal place alongside nerve gas and radioactive wastes and PCBs and crack, and DDT and Agent Orange and the AIDS virus, and on and on.

Not while I'm President. In the words of Patrick Henry: *If this be treason, make the most of it.*

Am I proposing a redistribution of wealth? You bet, since the wealth is being redistributed in any case, and often most crazily, and against the national interest. Am I proposing that we tax and tax and spend and spend? Yes, I am. Virtually every transaction is being skimmed already, and some private persons have done this at such confiscatory rates as to become as rich as smaller sovereign nations in a few years' time. And they spend and spend. On what? On what?

Ah, me.

Am I proposing an enormous public works program? How else might we describe our military-industrial complex, so mistrusted by that great Republican, General of the Armies Dwight David Eisenhower, when he himself became our President? With your encouragement I want to take much of the money now going into that public works program and invest it instead in the arts of peace, the noblest of which are public health and education.

Who says otherwise? And why?　　　　　■

THE WEIMAR
QUESTIONS? (1998)

The city of Weimar, the Goethe Institute and the European literary magazine Lettre Internationale are co-sponsoring an essay contest in conjunction with Weimar's role as Europe's cultural capital for 1999. According to the New York Times, the organizers "invited some 900 philosophers, historians, scientists, artists and assorted luminaries from around the world to propose topics." After considering more than 113 replies, the judges chose not one but two questions for the world's thinkers to ponder. They are:

Liberating the Future from the Past?
Liberating the Past from the Future?

*The Weimar contest asks participants for a maximum
of 10,500 words on these pressing issues. After some re-
flection, we decided there must be metaphysicians out
there who could do the job in about 500 words, so we invited a number of them to take up the challenge. We also
asked them to be philosophical about our inability to offer
a first prize to match Weimar's $28,000. Instead, the
author judged best by our in-house committee of logical
positivists will win a first edition of Christopher Isher-
wood's Berlin Stories.*

T he old university town of Weimar, which has
now called attention to itself by proposing two
questions for thinkers of the world to ponder, was
once the home of the great poets and dramatists
Goethe (1749-1832) and Schiller (1759-1805), a long time
ago. Goethe is best known for his reworking of the legend
of Faust, an old scholar who sold his soul to the Devil in
exchange for youth, love and knowledge. And a lot of people
know Schiller wrote "Ode to Joy," which Beethoven set to
tremendously romantic music.

Because of them, Weimar was at one time the scene
of passionate debates about how poets might best respond
to the intellectual earthquake, largely inspired by eigh-
teenth-century advances in science, that has come to be

known as the Age of Reason. Such an academic conundrum can scarcely set off a tempest in a teapot nowadays. Nor can a performance of Goethe's *Faust*, or a recitation of "Ode to Joy" without music, thrill many modern souls.

But Weimar, population only 65,000, the same population as Schenectady, New York, is in 1998 remembered by millions, and the heck with poetry, as having been the feeble, democratic capital of a ruined Germany after World War I—before the shit hit the fan—before the permanently unforgettable and unforgivable atrociousness of the Hitler era and World War II. "Weimar," unlike "Schenectady," has become an unfortunately generic place name, as has its neighboring hamlet "Buchenwald."

So when Weimar offers two questions to the world, one cannot help but consider their source. When that is done, they almost inevitably revise themselves as follows: "Liberating Weimar from the Past? Liberating the Past from Weimar?"

"Unring the bell?"   ∎

AFTERWORD
GOD BLESS YOU, MR. VONNEGUT (2004)

Excerpted from a speech by the late John Leonard at a birthday celebration for Kurt Vonnegut. Leonard, former literary editor of The Nation and former editor of the New York Times Book Review, was also a friend of Vonnegut.

L ike Mark Twain and Abraham Lincoln, even when he's funny, Kurt Vonnegut is depressed.... His own country has driven him to furious despair with its globocop belligerence, its contempt for civil liberties, and its holy war on the poor: "Mobilize the reserves! Privatize the public schools! Attack Iraq!

Cut health care! Tap everybody's telephone! Cut taxes on the rich! Build a trillion-dollar missile shield! Fuck habeas corpus and the Sierra Club… and kiss my ass!" The novelist/pacifist/socialist/humanist who has smoked unfiltered Pall Malls since he was 12 is suing the tobacco company that makes them because, "for many years now, right on the package, Brown and Williamson have promised to kill me. But I am now 82. Thanks a lot, you dirty rats. The last thing I ever wanted was to be alive when the three most powerful people on the whole planet would be named Bush, Dick and Colon."

So, although he does mention Jerry Garcia, Madame Blavatsky, Rush Limbaugh, and Saul Steinberg ("who, like everybody else I know, is dead now"), besides wonderfully observing that "Hamlet's situation is the same as Cinderella's, except that the sexes are reversed," he can't help but notice that "human beings, past and present, have trashed the joint," and that we are stuck in "a really scary reality show" called "C-Students from Yale." Thus he reiterates what Abraham Lincoln said about American imperialism in Mexico, what Mark Twain said about American imperialism in the Philippines, and what a visiting Martian anthropologist said about American culture in general in a novel Vonnegut hasn't finished writing yet: "What can it possibly be about blow jobs and golf?"…

Once upon a very long time ago I asked him to review a Joe Heller novel for *The New York Times*. This is how he concluded his essay on *Something Happened*: "I say that this is the most memorable, and therefore the most permanent variation on a familiar theme, and that it says baldly what the other variations only implied, what the other variations tried with desperate sentimentality not to imply: That many lives, judged by the standards of the people who live them, are simply not worth living."

Some of those variations are his own. A character in *Slaughterhouse 5* tells a psychiatrist: "I think you guys are going to have to come up with a lot of wonderful new lies, or people just aren't going to want to go on living." The novelist himself tells us in *Palm Sunday* about seeing a Marcel Ophuls film that included pictures from the Dresden firebombing Vonnegut had lived through as a POW: "The Dresden atrocity," he then decides, "tremendously expensive and meticulously planned, was so meaningless, finally, that only one person on the entire planet got any benefit from it. I am that person. I wrote this book, which earned a lot of money for me and made my reputation, such as it is. One way or another, I got two or three dollars for every person killed. Some business I'm in." In the same open vein, he wonders aloud in *Hocus Pocus*: "How is this for a definition of high art?... Making the most of the raw materials of futility."

Indeed. So it goes. Imagine that. And yet there isn't a person in this room who hasn't experienced a personal Kurt kindness, or been kissed with grace by something in one of his novels, or both. The way he goes about his business has helped most of us to go on living, if only to find out what happens next. In *Slapstick* he insisted that even if we aren't "really very good at life," we must nonetheless, like Laurel and Hardy, "bargain in good faith" with our destinies. And he recommended instruction books on such bargaining: *Robert's Rules of Order*, the Bill of Rights and the 12 Steps of Alcoholics Anonymous. To these, *Jailbird* added two more how-to manuals: Lincoln's Second Inaugural, "with malice toward none," and the Sermon on the Mount. *Bluebeard* suggested Goethe's *Faust*, Picasso's *Guernica*, *Gulliver's Travels*, *Alice in Wonderland* and *Don Quixote*. Elsewhere, at the dedication of a library, he mentioned such "mantras" as *War and Peace*, *Origin of Species*, *Critique of Pure Reason*, *Madame Bovary* and *The Red Badge of Courage*; and in a speech to mental health professionals, such civilizing "fixtures" as Shakespeare's *Hamlet*, Beethoven's Fifth, Leonardo's *Mona Lisa*, Twain's *Huck Finn*, the Great Wall of China, the Leaning Tower of Pisa and the Sphinx.

What are these fixtures, mantras and manuals but attempts to articulate standards according to which life is worth living? We read him as the woman in *Jailbird* read the books of Starbuck, "the way a young cannibal might eat the hearts of brave old enemies. Their magic would become hers." Add to these his autumnal novel, *Hocus Pocus*, so prematurely valedictory, where the Civil War is far from over, the race war still rages and a class war between the dyslexic rich and the illiterate poor has just begun; where Eugene Debs Hartke, like Howard Campbell in *Mother Night* and Kilgore Trout in *Jailbird*, will go on trial for treason; where the novelist seems to say goodbye to American history and literature, to *Moby-Dick* and Walt Whitman, as if covering so much territory—from evolution to outer space, from Abstract Expressionism to Watergate, from Holocaust to Hirsoshima—had worn him out. But he came back to us, over the ice and through the fire.

That scary fire: Remembering how he looked in the hospital after he almost burned his house down, Billy Pilgrim this time smoked instead of smoking, and seeing him now in these bright lights, the black humorist in black tie, I think we are blessed. It's as if he had returned, in reverse, from Dresden, like those bombers of his in one of the loveliest passages in our literature: American planes, full of holes and wounded men and corpses, took off backwards from an air field in England. Over France, a few German fighters flew at them backwards, sucked bullets and shell fragments from some of the planes and crewmen… The formation flew backwards over a German city that was in flames.

The bombers opened their bomb bay doors, exerted a miraculous magnetism which shrunk the flames, gathered them into cylindrical steel containers, and lifted the containers into the bellies of the planes… When the bombers got back to base, the steel cylinders were taken from the racks and shipped back to the United States of America, where factories were operating day and night, dismantling the cylinders, separating the dangerous contents into minerals. Touchingly, it was mainly women who did this work. The minerals were then shipped to specialists in remote areas. It was their business to put them into the ground, to hide them cleverly, so they would never hurt anybody ever again.

My wish is for Kurt to enjoy his birthday as much as we have. Because then maybe he'd be happy. ∎

{END}